Malpractice Issues for CPAs

Steven M. Bragg

AccountingTools®

ISBN 978-1-64221-334-8

For more information about AccountingTools® products, visit our Web site at www.accountingtools.com.

Table of Contents

About the Author

Steven Bragg, CPA, has been the chief financial officer or controller of four companies, as well as a consulting manager at Ernst & Young. He received a master's degree in finance from Bentley College, an MBA from Babson College, and a Bachelor's degree in Economics from the University of Maine. He has been a two-time president of the Colorado Mountain Club, and is an avid alpine skier, mountain biker, and certified master diver. Mr. Bragg resides in Centennial, Colorado. He has written more than 300 books and courses, including *New Controller Guidebook*, *GAAP Guidebook*, and *Payroll Management*. He has also written *The Auditors* science fiction trilogy.

Steven maintains the accountingtools.com web site, which contains continuing professional education courses, the Accounting Best Practices podcast, and thousands of articles on accounting subjects.

Buy Additional AccountingTools Courses

AccountingTools offers more than 1,500 hours of CPE courses, with concentrations in accounting, auditing, finance, taxation, and ethics. Related courses that you might like include:

- Guide to Auditor Legal Liability
- How to Conduct an Audit Engagement
- The Audit Risk Model

Go to accountingtools.com/cpe to view these additional courses.

AccountingTools®

Malpractice Issues for CPAs

Introduction

One of the main concerns for any practicing CPA is being accused of malpractice. A successful claim can be ruinous, possibly resulting in a large payout, plus regulatory fines, a suspended license, a ruined reputation, and the loss of customers. In this book, we discuss the nature of malpractice claims, what triggers them, and how to prevent them.

What is Malpractice?

Malpractice in the accounting profession refers to a situation in which a CPA or other accounting professional fails to perform their duties in accordance with the applicable standards of care, competence, and ethical conduct, resulting in harm or financial loss to a client or third party. This may arise from negligence, such as errors in financial statement preparation or tax filings, or from intentional misconduct, such as misrepresentation or participation in fraudulent schemes. Malpractice encompasses both civil liability—through claims of breach of contract or tort—and, in some cases, criminal liability when willful misconduct is involved. Courts and professional boards evaluate malpractice by comparing the accountant's conduct to what a reasonably prudent professional would have done under similar circumstances, as defined by professional standards, regulations, and relevant case law.

The Role of Professional Judgment and Fiduciary Responsibility

CPAs are held to high standards of competence and integrity due to the critical role they play in financial reporting, auditing, and advisory services. In the context of malpractice claims, two core principles are often examined: professional judgment and fiduciary responsibility. These principles not only guide a CPA's daily decisions but also serve as key benchmarks in legal proceedings that determine whether a practitioner acted within the bounds of professional conduct.

Professional judgment refers to the application of relevant knowledge, experience, and ethical standards in making decisions or providing opinions in complex or ambiguous situations. CPAs frequently operate in environments where the applicable rules, such as Generally Accepted Accounting Principles (GAAP) or auditing standards, require interpretation and contextualization. The exercise of sound professional judgment is essential in selecting appropriate accounting methods, evaluating internal controls, or identifying potential material misstatements. In a malpractice case, courts and regulatory bodies scrutinize whether a CPA's decisions align with what a reasonably prudent accountant would have done under similar circumstances. Poor or reckless judgment that leads to financial harm for a client may be considered evidence of negligence or incompetence.

Fiduciary responsibility, although more commonly associated with trustees or investment advisors, may arise for CPAs, depending on the nature of their client relationship. A fiduciary duty exists when a CPA is in a position of trust and confidence, acting on behalf of a client's best interests. This responsibility involves loyalty, full disclosure, confidentiality, and a duty to avoid conflicts of interest. For example, a CPA engaged to manage financial affairs, provide estate planning advice, or serve in an advisory capacity beyond traditional accounting may be deemed a fiduciary. In malpractice litigation, a breach of fiduciary duty can be asserted when a CPA fails to act with the utmost good faith, engages in self-dealing, or neglects to inform clients of material information that affects their interests.

Both professional judgment and fiduciary duty intersect in malpractice claims in that they establish the CPA's expected conduct. A failure to apply reasonable professional judgment may support claims of negligence, while a breach of fiduciary responsibility may constitute gross misconduct or intentional wrongdoing. In some cases, both theories are presented simultaneously to strengthen the plaintiff's position.

Furthermore, professional standards reinforce the importance of exercising due care and maintaining objectivity. These standards are often cited in court to demonstrate the baseline expectations for CPA behavior. Even when fiduciary status is not formally imposed, courts may assess the level of trust and dependency placed on a CPA when determining liability.

In sum, a CPA's professional judgment and fiduciary responsibility are central to both the delivery of competent services and the defense against malpractice allegations. Understanding and adhering to these principles not only helps CPAs reduce their legal exposure but also fosters trust and credibility in their professional relationships.

The Importance of Understanding Legal Exposure

Understanding legal exposure is critically important for CPAs who are subject to malpractice claims, as it directly influences how they manage risk, structure their services, and uphold professional standards. *Legal exposure* refers to the potential for civil or regulatory liability arising from a CPA's professional conduct. Given the fiduciary nature of many client relationships and the complexity of financial environments, CPAs must be keenly aware of how their actions or failures to act can result in allegations of negligence, breach of contract, or even fraud.

Malpractice claims often arise from errors or omissions in financial reporting, audit failures, tax advice, or a failure to detect fraud. CPAs may be held liable not only to their direct clients but also to third parties, such as investors, lenders, or regulatory agencies, who rely on their work. Understanding the scope of this exposure helps CPAs anticipate areas of vulnerability and adopt strategies to mitigate the risk, such as thorough documentation, client communication, and peer review processes.

A key component of understanding legal exposure is recognizing the legal standards that govern a CPA's conduct. Malpractice claims typically rely on the concept of *reasonable care*, which is whether the CPA acted in a manner consistent with what another reasonably prudent professional would have done under similar circumstances. Failure to meet this standard can result in liability for damages. CPAs must be familiar with applicable professional standards, such as those issued by the AICPA, PCAOB, or IRS, as these are often used to assess whether a breach occurred.

Moreover, legal exposure includes contractual obligations. When a CPA enters into an engagement with a client, the terms of the engagement letter create specific duties. If a CPA fails to deliver promised services or deviates from agreed-upon terms without cause, they may face a breach of contract claim. These claims can proceed even in the absence of gross negligence, making it imperative for CPAs to carefully define their scope of work and avoid taking on obligations they cannot reasonably fulfill.

Another critical element of legal exposure is liability for third-party reliance. Courts have increasingly recognized that CPAs may owe duties to non-clients in cases where it was foreseeable that these parties would rely on the CPA's work product, such as audited financial statements. This broadens potential exposure and heightens the importance of issuing disclaimers, adhering to professional standards, and maintaining independence.

Finally, understanding legal exposure allows CPAs to take proactive steps such as securing professional liability insurance, implementing quality control procedures, and staying current with their continuing professional education. These risk management practices not only help prevent malpractice claims but also demonstrate due diligence and good faith in the event of litigation.

In summary, understanding legal exposure enables CPAs to identify risks, adhere to legal and ethical obligations, and develop protective strategies that limit their liability. It is an essential aspect of professional practice that enhances both compliance and client trust, while also reducing the likelihood and severity of malpractice claims.

Overview of Litigation Trends Affecting CPAs

Litigation trends affecting CPAs have evolved significantly in recent years, driven by regulatory changes, economic volatility, and increasing expectations for professional accountability. These trends reflect a growing willingness of clients, investors, and regulatory bodies to hold CPAs legally responsible for errors, omissions, and perceived failures in judgment. As a result, CPAs must stay informed about litigation risks to proactively manage their professional liability and maintain compliance with changing legal standards.

One prominent trend is the rise in third-party lawsuits. Traditionally, CPAs were primarily liable to their clients; however, courts have increasingly allowed third parties, such as investors, creditors, and shareholders, to pursue legal action when they rely on a CPA's work product, particularly audited financial statements. This expansion of liability has heightened the stakes for CPAs, especially in assurance services, where financial statements serve as the foundation for economic decisions. To manage this risk, CPAs must exercise diligence in disclosure practices, documentation, and compliance with applicable standards.

Another notable trend involves heightened scrutiny from regulatory bodies, such as the Securities and Exchange Commission and state boards of accountancy. These agencies have increased enforcement activity in areas such as audit quality, independence violations, and ethical misconduct. CPAs working with public companies face particular exposure, as PCAOB inspections and enforcement actions may lead to civil penalties, license suspension, or professional sanctions, even in cases where no client complaint has been filed.

The complexity of modern business transactions has also contributed to litigation risk. CPAs now advise on issues such as mergers, tax strategies, and financial instruments that require advanced knowledge and professional judgment. With this complexity comes a higher potential for misinterpretation, mistakes, or disputes over the scope of services being provided. Clients may allege that CPAs gave misleading advice, failed to identify material issues, or inadequately disclosed financial risks. In such cases, even well-intentioned professionals can become the target of malpractice claims.

Additionally, fraud detection continues to be a common theme in CPA litigation. Although CPAs are not guarantors of fraud prevention, plaintiffs often argue that a CPA should have detected fraudulent activity during an audit or review. High-profile accounting scandals have raised public expectations regarding a CPA's role in uncovering irregularities, making it more likely that litigants will assert a failure to detect fraud as a basis for negligence.

Lastly, technology and cybersecurity concerns are creating new litigation risks. CPAs who handle sensitive client data or offer IT advisory services may face legal consequences for data breaches, poor cybersecurity controls, or inadequate disclosures about digital risks. As cyberattacks and privacy laws increase in prominence, the legal exposure in this area is expected to grow.

In summary, litigation trends affecting CPAs reveal a profession under increasing legal and regulatory pressure. Expanding third-party liability, regulatory enforcement, complex client engagements, rising fraud claims, and technology-related risks all underscore the need for CPAs to remain vigilant, informed, and proactive in managing legal exposure and safeguarding professional integrity.

EXAMPLE

The Supreme Court of New York County heard a dispute between Island Consolidated and its affiliated companies against the CPA firm Grassi & Co. The plaintiffs had hired Grassi in 2015 to manage their sales tax compliance and relied on the firm's guidance for several years. According to the lawsuit, Grassi & Co. provided tax advice that was materially flawed, leading the clients to incur significant financial consequences, including back taxes, penalties, interest, and the loss of future business opportunities.

The central issue in the case was not merely whether an error had occurred, but whether Grassi's conduct rose to the level of gross negligence. The plaintiffs alleged that Grassi & Co. had knowingly failed to provide the same accurate sales tax guidance that it had extended to other clients in similar industries. More troubling, they claimed that the firm later attempted to conceal the mistake by falsely asserting that a change in tax law in 2020 had caused the problem, when in fact the issue had been present from the outset.

Grassi & Co. moved to dismiss the lawsuit on several grounds, including procedural deficiencies, the statute of limitations, and the assertion that the complaint failed to state a claim for either ordinary or gross negligence. However, the court rejected these arguments, holding that the plaintiffs' allegations, if proven true, were sufficient to support a claim not only for professional malpractice but also for gross negligence. The judge emphasized that under New York law, gross negligence implies more than simple carelessness; it involves a reckless disregard for a client's interests or intentional wrongdoing.

The court found that the plaintiffs had met the required legal threshold at the pleading stage by offering detailed factual claims that suggested a knowing failure to act and a potential effort to mislead the client. Although no final judgment has been rendered, the decision to allow the case to proceed significantly raised the stakes for Grassi & Co., as a finding of gross negligence can result in punitive damages and reputational harm beyond that associated with typical malpractice claims.

This case serves as a cautionary tale for CPAs. While mistakes may occur in the course of professional services, the way those mistakes are handled can dramatically influence legal outcomes. The allegation that the firm attempted to cover up its error transformed what might have been a straightforward negligence case into a more serious legal challenge. For practitioners, the Grassi case underscores the importance of transparency, ethical responsibility, and proactive communication when errors arise. In a legal landscape where clients and third parties are increasingly willing to litigate, this case highlights the necessity of maintaining both technical competence and professional integrity at all times.

Sources of a CPA's Duty of Care

A CPA has a duty of care when conducting work for a client. In this section, we address the common law origins of the duty of care, how this concept has been incorporated into the AICPA Code of Professional Conduct, and the concepts of ordinary negligence and professional negligence.

Common Law Origins of the Duty of Care

The duty of care owed by CPAs originates from the principles of common law, particularly in tort and contract law. At its core, the duty of care requires CPAs to exercise the level of skill, competence, and diligence that a reasonably prudent accountant would employ under similar circumstances. This obligation, though codified in professional standards today, was first shaped by judicial decisions over decades of litigation concerning professional negligence.

In tort law, the concept of *duty of care* emerged as a foundational element of negligence claims. Courts have long held that professionals, including accountants, owe a duty to their clients to perform services with due care. This relationship was first defined in narrow terms, recognizing liability only to parties in privity of contract. However, over time, courts began to expand the scope of this duty in response to the increasing reliance of third parties on financial statements and professional advice. A landmark case in this evolution was *Ultramares Corporation v. Touche* (1931), where the New York Court of Appeals acknowledged the potential for third-party reliance but refused to impose unlimited liability on accountants. The decision established that liability to third parties required a "relationship so close as to approach privity," a standard later broadened by subsequent rulings.

From a contractual standpoint, a CPA's duty of care is embedded in the terms of engagement agreements with clients. These contracts outline the specific services to be rendered and form the basis for evaluating whether a breach occurred. Failure to meet the expectations set forth in such agreements can result in breach of contract claims, even if no independent tort has been committed.

As the accounting profession evolved, courts increasingly recognized that CPAs, due to their expertise and the public trust placed in their work, are held to high expectations. Modern interpretations of the duty of care require CPAs to follow established professional standards, such as Generally Accepted Auditing Standards (GAAS) or Statements on Standards for Tax Services (SSTS), depending on the engagement type. Deviation from these standards, especially where damages result, may be deemed a failure to exercise due care.

In sum, the duty of care for CPAs has deep common law roots, shaped by tort and contract principles and informed by judicial precedent. It serves as a critical measure for professional conduct and remains central to malpractice claims in both client and third-party contexts.

AICPA Code of Professional Conduct

The AICPA Code of Professional Conduct serves as a foundational framework that guides CPAs in upholding their professional responsibilities, including the duty of care. While the Code encompasses a broad range of ethical principles, the duty of care is most directly addressed through the principles of due professional care, competence, and professional behavior. These principles shape how CPAs are expected to conduct themselves in performing their services and serve as benchmarks in malpractice evaluations.

Due care, as outlined in the Code's *Principles* section, requires CPAs to observe the profession's technical and ethical standards, strive continuously to improve their competence and quality of services, and discharge professional responsibility to the best of their ability. This principle emphasizes the importance of diligence, thoughtful judgment, and a commitment to quality in every engagement. CPAs are expected to act with the same level of care and skill that a reasonably prudent professional would apply in similar circumstances.

The *General Standards Rule* further reinforces the duty of care by requiring CPAs to undertake only those professional services that they can reasonably expect to complete with competence. The rule mandates proper planning, supervision, and the exercise of professional judgment. This means CPAs must not only possess the necessary skills but also remain current with relevant laws, regulations, and standards. Failing to meet these standards may expose the CPA to disciplinary action by the AICPA or state boards and may also serve as evidence in a malpractice claim.

The *Compliance with Standards Rule* ensures that CPAs adhere to applicable technical standards issued by recognized bodies such as the AICPA, FASB, or PCAOB. Compliance with these standards is a core component of fulfilling the duty of care. Deviating from these standards without reasonable justification can be interpreted as negligence or misconduct.

Additionally, the Code requires CPAs to maintain objectivity and integrity in all engagements. These ethical imperatives support the duty of care by ensuring that CPAs provide unbiased, fact-based services and avoid conflicts of interest that might impair their professional judgment.

In conclusion, the AICPA Code of Professional Conduct provides a comprehensive ethical foundation that informs and supports a CPA's duty of care. By adhering to its principles and rules, CPAs demonstrate their commitment to high-quality service, ethical conduct, and professional accountability.

Engagement Letters and Client Expectations

Engagement letters play a vital role in defining the professional relationship between CPAs and their clients, particularly in the context of malpractice claims. These documents are more than formalities; they establish the scope, terms, and limitations of the services to be provided, helping manage client expectations and mitigate legal risk. When malpractice claims arise, courts often examine the engagement letter as a key piece of evidence to determine whether the CPA breached a duty or acted outside the agreed scope of work.

A well-drafted engagement letter clearly outlines the nature of the services to be rendered, as well as the responsibilities of both the CPA and the client. By delineating the specific tasks the CPA agrees to perform, the letter helps set realistic client expectations and protects against claims based on services the CPA did not agree to provide. For example, if a CPA is engaged solely to prepare tax returns, and the client later sues for failure to detect fraud in the company's books, the engagement letter can be used to show that fraud detection was outside the CPA's scope of responsibility.

The engagement letter also defines key elements such as timelines, fees, confidentiality terms, and any disclaimers or limitations of liability. Importantly, it may include language clarifying that the CPA's work does not constitute an audit or assurance service unless expressly stated. These provisions are crucial when clients misunderstand the nature or limitations of the services provided. Misaligned expectations can lead to allegations of negligence or breach of contract if the client believes the CPA was responsible for tasks or results that were not part of the agreement.

In malpractice litigation, the engagement letter is frequently used to assess whether a duty existed, whether it was breached, and whether damages resulted. If a CPA can demonstrate that they complied with the terms outlined in the letter and followed applicable professional standards, they are in a stronger position to defend against malpractice allegations. Conversely, the absence of a written engagement letter may allow clients to argue that implied duties existed, increasing the CPA's exposure to liability.

In sum, engagement letters are essential tools for risk management. They serve to align client expectations with professional obligations, document the scope of services, and provide a basis for defending against unfounded malpractice claims. For CPAs, careful use of engagement letters is a key safeguard against legal disputes and reputational harm.

Comparison of Ordinary Negligence and Professional Negligence

In the context of malpractice claims against CPAs, it is important to distinguish between ordinary negligence and professional negligence, as each carries different implications for liability and defense. Both concepts involve a failure to exercise reasonable care, but they differ in scope, legal interpretation, and professional standards.

Ordinary negligence refers to a general failure to act with the care that a reasonably prudent person would use in similar circumstances. This form of negligence does not require specialized knowledge or skill and can apply to any individual, regardless of profession. For example, a CPA who misplaces client documents or forgets to file a return on time without a valid reason may be liable for ordinary negligence. The standard used to evaluate this conduct is what a layperson or a non-specialist would reasonably be expected to do under similar circumstances.

Professional negligence, on the other hand, involves a failure to exercise the level of care, skill, and diligence that a reasonably prudent CPA would exhibit under comparable professional circumstances. It applies when the alleged misconduct arises from the CPA's performance of specialized services such as audits, tax planning, or financial consulting. For instance, if a CPA fails to detect material misstatements during an audit due to a lack of proper testing or documentation, that failure would be evaluated under professional negligence standards. The court would examine whether the CPA's actions met the expectations defined by professional standards.

The key difference lies in the standard of care. Professional negligence holds CPAs to a higher, industry-specific standard because of their education, training, and the public trust placed in their work. As a result, expert testimony is often required in professional negligence cases to establish what a competent CPA would have done in similar circumstances. In contrast, ordinary negligence cases may not require expert input because the alleged conduct is easier for jurors or judges to understand without specialized knowledge.

In malpractice claims, this distinction affects how liability is proven and what defenses are available. A CPA accused of ordinary negligence may argue that their actions were reasonable under general standards, while in a professional negligence claim, the defense must show adherence to recognized accounting principles and ethical obligations.

Ultimately, understanding this distinction is essential for CPAs to assess legal exposure and ensure compliance with both general and professional duties of care.

Common Law Causes of Action Against CPAs

CPAs are held to high professional and ethical standards due to the trust placed in them by clients, investors, regulators, and the public. When a CPA fails to meet these standards, they may be subject to legal claims under common law. These claims fall into several well-established categories, including negligence, breach of contract, fraud and misrepresentation, constructive fraud, and breach of fiduciary duty. Each cause of action involves distinct legal elements and consequences, and understanding these distinctions is critical for both practitioners and those who rely on their work. We cover these concepts separately in the following sub-sections.

Negligence

Negligence is the most common basis for malpractice claims against CPAs. Under common law, negligence occurs when a CPA fails to exercise the level of care, skill, and diligence that a reasonably competent professional would apply in similar circumstances, resulting in harm to the client or a foreseeable third party.

To establish negligence, a plaintiff must prove that:

- The CPA owed a duty of care
- The CPA breached that duty
- The breach caused harm
- The plaintiff suffered actual damages

The duty of care is typically defined by the standards of the accounting profession, including guidelines issued by the AICPA, PCAOB, or IRS, depending on the engagement. Examples of negligence might include failure to detect material errors in financial statements, improper tax advice resulting in penalties, or inadequate documentation during an audit.

Breach of Contract

A *breach of contract* claim arises when a CPA fails to perform services as outlined in a formal agreement, typically an engagement letter. Unlike negligence, breach of contract does not require a showing of professional misconduct, just a failure to meet agreed-upon obligations.

The plaintiff must demonstrate the following:

- A valid contract existed
- The CPA failed to perform as promised
- The client suffered damages as a result

For example, if a CPA agrees to complete an audit by a certain date but fails to do so, thereby causing the client to miss a financing deadline, the client may seek damages for the breach. Importantly, breach of contract claims are limited to the parties involved in the agreement; third parties typically cannot sue unless they are intended beneficiaries of the contract.

While negligence and breach of contract may overlap, courts sometimes distinguish between the two to determine what damages are recoverable and what defenses apply. A contract may also include limitation of liability clauses or arbitration provisions that alter how claims are handled.

Fraud and Misrepresentation

Fraud is a serious allegation that involves intentional wrongdoing. A CPA may be liable for fraud if they knowingly make a false statement of material fact, with the intent to deceive, and a party reasonably relies on that statement to their detriment.

To prove fraud, the plaintiff must establish the following:

- A false representation of a material fact
- Knowledge of the falsity or reckless disregard for the truth
- Intent to induce reliance
- Justifiable reliance by the plaintiff
- Resulting damages

An example would be a CPA knowingly certifying inaccurate financial statements to help a client obtain a loan or investment. If the third party relies on these false statements and incurs financial loss, the CPA could be liable for fraud. Courts impose heavy penalties for fraudulent conduct, and liability can include punitive damages.

Fraud claims differ from negligence in that intent is central. While negligence involves a failure to exercise care, fraud involves a deliberate decision to mislead. Consequently, fraud claims require a higher burden of proof and more detailed pleading requirements in litigation.

Constructive Fraud

Constructive fraud, also known as negligent misrepresentation, is a less severe but still serious form of misconduct. It involves false statements made without the intent to deceive, but under circumstances where the CPA had a duty to know the truth and failed to exercise reasonable care.

The elements of constructive fraud typically include the following:

- A false statement or omission
- Made negligently or with gross disregard for the truth
- In the context of a fiduciary or confidential relationship
- Upon which the plaintiff justifiably relied
- Resulting in damages

Constructive fraud often arises in audit or advisory engagements where the CPA issues a report without exercising due professional care, resulting in materially misleading financial information. While no intent to deceive is required, the law treats the CPA's conduct as so reckless that it warrants heightened liability.

This type of claim blurs the line between negligence and fraud, serving as a middle ground in cases where the facts suggest egregious carelessness, but not intentional misconduct. Courts often apply constructive fraud when a fiduciary relationship exists, reinforcing the CPA's heightened duty of trust.

Breach of Fiduciary Duty

A fiduciary duty arises when a CPA occupies a position of trust and confidence, often involving discretionary authority over a client's financial matters. Not all CPA-client relationships qualify as fiduciary; however, when they do, the CPA must act with utmost loyalty, disclose all material facts, and avoid self-dealing or conflicts of interest.

To succeed in a breach of fiduciary duty claim, the plaintiff must show the following:

- The existence of a fiduciary relationship
- A breach of the duty of loyalty or care
- Resulting harm to the client

Examples include situations where a CPA serves as a financial advisor, trustee, or estate administrator and acts in their own interest rather than the client's. Even accepting undisclosed commissions or failing to disclose conflicts of interest can lead to such claims.

Breach of fiduciary duty claims are especially damaging because they often imply willful misconduct or exploitation of trust. Remedies may include not only compensatory damages but also equitable relief such as disgorgement of fees or rescission of transactions.

In many malpractice cases, plaintiffs allege both negligence and breach of fiduciary duty to cover alternative theories of liability. Courts analyze these claims separately, as fiduciary breaches may arise even in the absence of negligence, particularly when involving dishonesty or concealment.

Conclusion

The common law causes of action against CPAs reflect the diverse ways a CPA can be held accountable for professional misconduct. Each claim requires a different level of proof and imposes varying degrees of liability. While negligence and breach of contract are the most frequently litigated, fraud-related claims and fiduciary breaches carry more severe reputational and financial consequences.

For CPAs, awareness of these potential legal exposures is essential for practicing with care, adhering to professional standards, maintaining clear client communication, and documenting engagements thoroughly. Proper risk management, such as engagement letters, liability insurance, and ongoing education, plays a vital role in preventing legal disputes and upholding the trust placed in the profession.

Key Case Law Defining Reasonable CPA Behavior

There have been many malpractice cases over the years, but only a few of them are considered landmark cases, because the underlying principles set forth in them by the courts have been used subsequently to determine the outcomes of cases. These landmark cases are noted in the following sub-sections.

Ultramares Corp. v. Touche

The *Ultramares Corp. v. Touche* case (1931) is a decision by the New York Court of Appeals that significantly influenced the scope of accountant liability to third parties. In this case, Touche, Niven & Co., a public accounting firm, had audited the financial statements of Fred Stern & Co., a client engaged in wholesale business. The firm issued multiple copies of the certified financial statements, knowing they would be used to secure loans. Ultramares Corporation, relying on the certified statements, extended substantial credit to Stern, which subsequently declared bankruptcy. When it was revealed that the financial statements were materially misstated, Ultramares sued Touche for negligence and fraud.

The central legal question was whether an accountant could be held liable for ordinary negligence to a third party (Ultramares) who was not in privity of contract but relied on the accountant's certification. The court, led by Chief Judge Benjamin Cardozo, ruled that while an accountant could be liable for fraud or gross negligence, they could not be held liable for ordinary negligence to third parties lacking a contractual or near-privity relationship. Cardozo famously warned against exposing professionals to "liability in an indeterminate amount for an indeterminate time to an indeterminate class."

The court introduced the concept of "privity" or near-privity as a threshold for imposing liability. To establish near-privity, there must be a direct relationship or communication between the accountant and the third party, indicating that the accountant knew the third party would rely on their work. In the Ultramares case, while Touche may have known their report would be circulated, there was no direct contact or understanding that Ultramares would rely on it, thus failing to meet the near-privity standard.

This case is significant because it set a boundary on accountants' liability for negligence, protecting them from open-ended exposure to third-party claims while preserving liability for fraud or gross misconduct. It shaped future rulings and legal standards by distinguishing between ordinary negligence (which does not give rise to third-party claims without privity) and actionable misconduct (such as fraud), which can lead to broader liability. As a result, Ultramares became a foundational case in professional liability law, particularly for auditors, reinforcing the idea that professionals owe their primary duty to the client and not to an undefined public.

Credit Alliance v. Arthur Andersen

The *Credit Alliance Corp. v. Arthur Andersen & Co.* (1985) is a New York Court of Appeals case that further refined the standard for when accountants can be held liable to third parties for negligent misrepresentation. The case arose when Credit Alliance, a lending institution, extended significant loans to a client based on audited financial statements prepared by Arthur Andersen. When the client defaulted and the financial statements were revealed to be materially inaccurate, Credit Alliance sued Arthur Andersen for negligence. The key legal question was whether Arthur Andersen could be held liable to a third party (Credit Alliance) with whom it had no direct contractual relationship.

The court reaffirmed the general rule established in *Ultramares Corp. v. Touche*, holding that an accountant's liability to third parties for negligence is limited to those with whom the accountant has a relationship approaching privity. However, *Credit Alliance* clarified and expanded the criteria necessary to establish such a relationship, setting out a three-part test for near-privity: (1) the accountant must have been aware that the financial statements were to be used for a particular purpose or transaction by a known party; (2) there must have been conduct by the accountant linking them to the third party, showing the accountant's understanding that the third party would rely on the statements; and (3) the third party must have relied on the statements in connection with the specified purpose.

In this case, the court concluded that Credit Alliance did not meet these requirements. While Arthur Andersen may have known its audit would be used generally for financial purposes, there was no evidence of direct communication or conduct establishing that Arthur Andersen was aware Credit Alliance specifically would rely on the audit. As such, the court denied recovery for ordinary negligence, although it left open the possibility of a claim for fraud.

The *Credit Alliance* decision is significant because it clarified how close the relationship between an accountant and a third party must be to create liability for negligent misrepresentation. It rejected the broader "foreseeable reliance" approach, under which accountants could be held liable to any party who might reasonably rely on their work. Instead, it emphasized a narrower approach requiring clear awareness, intent, and connection.

Rusch Factors, Inc. v. Levin

The *Rusch Factors, Inc. v. Levin* case (1968) marked a significant departure from the restrictive privity requirement established in earlier cases such as *Ultramares* by embracing the "reasonable foreseeability" standard for auditor liability to third parties. In this case, Rusch Factors, a commercial finance company, sued accountant Levin for negligence after relying on financial statements he had prepared for a client in connection with a loan. The statements were materially inaccurate, and the borrower defaulted, causing financial loss to Rusch.

The primary issue before the United States District Court for the District of Rhode Island was whether Levin, as the accountant, could be held liable to a third party (Rusch) who was not in privity of contract with him but had relied on his work. The court ruled in favor of Rusch, adopting a broader view of liability based on the principle of *reasonable foreseeability*. The court reasoned that if it was reasonably foreseeable to the accountant that a third party would rely on the financial statements for a particular purpose, then the accountant owed a duty of care to that third party, even absent a direct contractual relationship.

The court emphasized that Levin knew his audit would be used to obtain financing, and it was reasonably foreseeable that a finance company such as Rusch would rely on the statements. Thus, the court found that Levin owed a duty of care to Rusch and could be held liable for negligent misrepresentation. Importantly, this approach focuses not on the existence of a near-privity relationship but rather on whether the reliance by the third party was reasonably foreseeable to the accountant at the time the audit was performed.

The *Rusch Factors* decision significantly expanded the potential liability of accountants and rejected the narrow confines of the privity or near-privity rule. By adopting the foreseeability test, it aligned with the broader tort law principle that professionals should be liable for harm caused to foreseeable users of their services, especially when their work is intended to influence financial decisions.

This case became an early example of a jurisdiction moving toward greater third-party protection and has influenced subsequent decisions in other states. However, not all courts have followed this path; many have preferred the more restrictive approach set in *Ultramares* and reaffirmed in *Credit Alliance*. Nonetheless, *Rusch Factors* remains a foundational case in the debate over accountant liability and third-party reliance.

Bily v. Arthur Young & Co.

Bily v. Arthur Young & Co. (1992) is a decision by the California Supreme Court that addressed the scope of an auditor's liability to third parties and sought to balance the competing public policy interests of accountability and limiting excessive litigation risk for accounting firms. The case involved a lawsuit by investors who relied on financial statements audited by Arthur Young & Co. in making investment decisions. When the company failed and fraud was uncovered, the investors sued the auditors for negligent misrepresentation.

The central legal issue was whether auditors should be liable to third parties who were not clients but relied on the audit in a foreseeable way. The court acknowledged the arguments in favor of extending liability to protect investors and creditors who depend on audited financial statements. However, it ultimately rejected the broad foreseeability standard and refused to impose general tort liability on auditors for negligent misrepresentation to third parties.

Instead, the court held that auditors owe a duty of care only to their clients and to a limited class of third parties for whose benefit the auditor specifically intended the audit to be used and who actually relied on it. This aligns more closely with the "actual knowledge" or "intended user" test, rather than the expansive "foreseeable user" rule followed in some other jurisdictions like in *Rusch Factors*.

The *Bily* court emphasized several public policy considerations in its decision. First, auditors do not have control over how their reports are used once disseminated, and exposing them to broad liability could lead to excessive caution or withdrawal from high-risk clients. Second, imposing unlimited liability might distort the function of audits, which are intended to serve as a reasonable assurance, not an absolute guarantee, of accuracy. Third, the court noted that clients, not third parties, are in the best position to control the audit process and ensure quality through contractual terms and oversight.

Significantly, the court distinguished between fraud and negligence. While it upheld potential liability for intentional misrepresentation or fraud, it concluded that imposing negligence liability to an open-ended class of third parties would be unfair and economically burdensome.

Bily v. Arthur Young thus represents a middle ground: it holds auditors accountable to known and intended users of their reports, but limits exposure to an undefined public. It remains a key precedent for balancing investor protection with the practical limits of professional responsibility.

Summary

The application of case law in malpractice claims continues to shape the legal environment in which CPAs operate. Foundational cases such as *Ultramares Corp. v. Touche, Credit Alliance v. Arthur Andersen, Rusch Factors v. Levin,* and *Bily v. Arthur Young* have laid the groundwork for defining the extent of a CPA's liability, particularly concerning third-party claims, professional negligence, and the standards of duty of care. These rulings remain highly relevant in today's accounting profession, where the demand for reliable financial information intersects with increased litigation risk.

Modern CPA practices must navigate liability exposure based on how courts interpret "duty of care." *Ultramares* introduced the principle that CPAs are not liable for ordinary negligence to third parties unless there is privity or a relationship approaching privity. This protects auditors from open-ended liability but still holds them accountable for fraud or gross negligence. *Credit Alliance* refined this by providing a three-part test for near-privity, focusing on the accountant's awareness of the third party, intent to influence that party, and direct conduct establishing a link.

These principles are critical in the current landscape, where CPAs prepare financial reports not only for clients but also for use by lenders, investors, regulators, and other stakeholders. Understanding whether liability extends to these parties depends on how closely the CPA's conduct aligns with the established case law criteria.

Some jurisdictions have adopted the *Rusch Factors* foreseeability test, exposing CPAs to broader liability by allowing third parties who were foreseeable users of the financial statements to bring negligence claims. This underscores the importance of understanding the legal climate in specific states or federal circuits in which a CPA operates.

In contrast, cases like *Bily v. Arthur Young* show how courts may prioritize limiting the liability of CPAs to avoid deterring professional services and to maintain a balanced public policy. The *Bily* court emphasized the need to prevent auditors from becoming insurers of financial accuracy for the entire public, a principle that remains vital as CPAs confront growing expectations for accuracy in financial disclosures and fraud detection.

Negligence Claims – Legal Elements and Risk Triggers

In this section, we cover the issues that a plaintiff must prove in court, the specific issues that can trigger a negligence claim, and the situations that are most likely to trigger malpractice claims.

Proving the Elements of Negligence in Court

To prove negligence in court against a CPA, a plaintiff must establish four key legal elements, which are duty, breach, causation, and damages. From the perspective of a CPA facing a negligence claim, understanding how each element is proven provides insight into the legal defenses that may be available. We expand upon these legal elements in the following bullet points:

- *Duty of care.* The first element requires showing that the CPA owed a legal duty of care to the plaintiff. This typically arises through a contractual engagement between the CPA and the client. However, under certain legal doctrines (such as *Credit Alliance v. Arthur Andersen*), the duty can extend to third parties if there is a relationship approaching privity; meaning the CPA was aware that the third party would rely on their work and intended for them to do so. Courts examine the engagement letter, scope of services, and communications to determine whether a duty existed. From a CPA's perspective, clearly defining the scope and limitations of service in the engagement letter can help limit who may be considered a foreseeable claimant.

- *Breach of duty.* The plaintiff must next demonstrate that the CPA breached their duty by failing to perform their services with the level of skill, care, and diligence expected of a reasonably competent professional under similar circumstances. This often involves expert testimony to show that the CPA deviated from the applicable professional standards. A CPA can defend against this claim by presenting evidence that their work followed applicable standards, procedures, and quality controls. Meticulous documentation of workpapers, professional judgments, and internal reviews are vital to refuting breach allegations.

- *Causation.* Causation has two components, which are actual cause and proximate cause. The plaintiff must prove that the CPA's breach directly caused the loss (actual cause) and that the loss was a foreseeable result of the CPA's conduct (proximate cause). Courts examine whether the CPA's work was a substantial factor in bringing about the harm. For example, if a CPA negligently failed to detect fraud that led to investor losses, the plaintiff must show the CPA's oversight caused those losses. CPAs can challenge causation by pointing to other factors, such as client misstatements, management override, or economic events outside the CPA's control.

- *Damages.* Finally, the plaintiff must prove actual financial harm resulting from the CPA's alleged negligence. Courts require clear evidence of quantifiable losses, such as lost investments, overpaid taxes, or reliance-based financial decisions. A CPA may defend this element by arguing that damages are speculative, unsubstantiated, or not attributable to the accountant's work.

In summary, a negligence case against a CPA hinges on whether the accountant owed a duty, breached that duty by failing to follow professional norms, and caused measurable harm. CPAs facing such claims should rely on strong engagement documentation, adherence to standards, clear communication, and expert defense to challenge each element effectively.

Documentation Failures and Audit Workpapers

In a negligence claim against a CPA, the quality and completeness of documentation and audit workpapers can play a pivotal role in either supporting the CPA's defense or undermining it. Audit documentation serves as the primary evidence that the CPA conducted their work in accordance with professional standards. When documentation is incomplete, inconsistent, or missing, it becomes significantly harder for the CPA to demonstrate that they exercised due professional care.

Audit workpapers provide a record of the procedures performed, evidence gathered, and conclusions reached during the course of an audit. They should clearly reflect risk assessments, analytical procedures, substantive tests, and how issues were resolved. In negligence litigation, these documents are often scrutinized by both plaintiffs and expert witnesses to determine whether the CPA met the applicable standard of care. A failure to document can create a presumption that a procedure was never performed, even if the CPA insists that it was. Courts and regulators alike tend to follow the principle: "If it's not documented, it didn't happen."

Documentation failures can also suggest broader deficiencies in the CPA's methodology, professionalism, or attention to detail. For example, if the audit file lacks evidence of follow-up on red flags or fails to contain sufficient information about management representations, this can be construed as a breach of professional duty. In such cases, plaintiffs may argue that the CPA's omissions allowed fraud or misstatement to go undetected, directly causing financial harm.

Moreover, workpapers are often used by expert witnesses to evaluate whether the CPA's work conformed to industry norms. If the file lacks essential components—such as confirmations, reconciliations, or internal control assessments—it becomes easier for the plaintiff's experts to argue that the CPA deviated from expected practices. Conversely, well-organized and thorough documentation enables the CPA to demonstrate that reasonable care and professional skepticism were applied, even if the outcome of the audit was flawed.

In some cases, documentation problems can also lead to regulatory penalties, thereby compounding the CPA's legal exposure. Destruction or alteration of audit workpapers post-engagement can trigger sanctions and potentially convert a negligence claim into a claim of gross negligence or misconduct.

In summary, documentation is not merely an administrative requirement; it is the CPA's best legal defense. Properly maintained workpapers can protect against allegations of negligence, while incomplete or deficient documentation can significantly increase the likelihood of liability in a malpractice claim.

Failure to Detect Fraud or Material Misstatement

The failure of a CPA to detect fraud or a material misstatement in financial statements can be a central issue in a negligence claim. While auditors are not expected to guarantee the absolute accuracy of financial statements, they are required to conduct audits in accordance with Generally Accepted Auditing Standards, which emphasize professional skepticism, risk assessment, and adequate evidential support. When a fraud or misstatement is later uncovered, and especially if it causes financial harm to a client or third party, the CPA's audit procedures come under intense scrutiny.

In negligence claims, the plaintiff must show that the CPA owed a duty of care, breached that duty, and caused quantifiable harm. A failure to detect fraud or a material misstatement is often used as evidence of a breach of duty. Courts and expert witnesses will examine whether the CPA adhered to audit standards, such as properly evaluating internal controls, performing analytical procedures, confirming transactions with third parties, and following up on anomalies. If the CPA failed to apply appropriate audit techniques or ignored warning signs, this can be viewed as a deviation from the professional standard of care, supporting the plaintiff's negligence claim.

Importantly, the magnitude of the undetected fraud or misstatement can influence the court's perception of the CPA's diligence. For instance, large-scale misstatements that went unnoticed over several periods may suggest systemic audit deficiencies. If red flags were present, such as inconsistent documentation, pressure from management, or unusual journal entries, but the CPA failed to investigate further, this weakens the defense and strengthens the case for negligence.

However, not every failure to detect fraud automatically constitutes negligence. Auditors are not infallible, and fraud can be actively concealed through collusion or forgery, making it inherently difficult to uncover. CPAs can defend themselves by demonstrating that they exercised professional skepticism, performed risk-based testing, documented their findings, and complied with the relevant standards, even if the fraud went undetected.

Causation is another critical factor. Plaintiffs must show that the CPA's failure to detect the fraud or misstatement directly caused their loss. CPAs can counter this by arguing that other factors, such as client misrepresentations, economic downturns, or independent investment decisions, were the true causes of the plaintiff's damages.

In summary, a CPA's failure to detect fraud or material misstatement can be highly damaging in a negligence lawsuit, especially if it reflects substandard audit procedures or ignored risk indicators. Thorough documentation, adherence to standards, and proactive risk assessment are essential defenses against such claims.

Inadequate Internal Controls Review

An inadequate review of a client's internal controls can significantly impact a negligence claim against a CPA, particularly in audit engagements. Internal control evaluation is a fundamental component of Generally Accepted Auditing Standards, especially under the risk assessment framework. Auditors are required to understand and assess a client's internal control environment to determine the nature, timing, and extent of audit procedures. Failure to conduct or document a proper review of internal controls can be interpreted as a breach of the CPA's professional duty and may support allegations of negligence.

When an auditor performs only a superficial or incomplete internal controls review, they may overlook material weaknesses or fail to design audit procedures that adequately address areas of high risk. This can result in undetected errors or fraud, especially in areas such as revenue recognition, inventory management, or related-party transactions. If such misstatements later come to light and cause harm, either to the client or third parties such as investors or creditors, the plaintiff may argue that the CPA's negligence in assessing internal controls was the root cause of the oversight.

Courts and expert witnesses in negligence cases often examine whether the CPA appropriately documented their understanding of internal controls, evaluated control risk, and modified audit procedures accordingly. If audit files lack walkthroughs, control testing results, or explanations of risk mitigation strategies, this can be viewed as a deviation from professional standards. Plaintiffs may use these omissions to demonstrate a failure to meet the duty of care owed by the CPA, particularly if the financial misstatement occurred in a process the auditor should have assessed as high risk.

Furthermore, under auditing standards, if control risk is assessed as low, the auditor must obtain evidence to support that assessment. If the CPA assumed controls were effective without sufficient testing, or failed to revise their risk assessment in light of emerging issues, this may constitute a breach. An inadequate internal controls review can also impact the auditor's ability to identify fraud risks, which can heighten the perception of negligence if fraud is subsequently discovered.

From a defense standpoint, a CPA may argue that certain controls were evaluated appropriately but later circumvented by management override or collusion – two limitations that even effective control systems cannot fully eliminate. However, without adequate documentation and risk analysis, such defenses are less persuasive.

In conclusion, an inadequate internal controls review can severely undermine a CPA's position in a negligence claim. It weakens the argument that the audit was conducted with due professional care and exposes the CPA to liability for failing to identify preventable misstatements or fraud risks. Robust documentation and compliance with control evaluation standards are essential safeguards.

Situations that Increase the Risk of Negligence Claims

Some of the more common situations that significantly increase the risk of negligence claims for a CPA are as follows:

- *Tax return preparation errors*. Mistakes such as incorrect income reporting, missed deductions, or filing inaccuracies can lead to client penalties, interest, or audits, often resulting in negligence claims if the errors stem from carelessness or a failure to follow applicable tax laws.
- *Failure to detect fraud or material misstatements*. When an audit misses fraudulent activity or material errors in financial statements, especially after obvious red flags were ignored, clients or third parties may claim the CPA did not exercise due professional care.
- *Inadequate internal control assessments*. Negligence claims may arise if a CPA fails to properly evaluate or document internal controls, leading to undetected financial irregularities or risks that could have been mitigated.

- *Failure to follow professional standards*. Deviating from accepted standards in audit, review, or compilation services can support claims that a CPA did not meet the standard of care required by the profession.
- *Lack of documentation*. Incomplete or missing audit workpapers, tax files, or engagement records make it difficult to defend the adequacy of services and can imply that critical procedures were not performed.
- *Overstepping the scope of engagement*. Providing advice or services beyond what was agreed to in the engagement letter, such as giving investment advice, can expose a CPA to liability for unanticipated outcomes or misinterpretations.
- *Client reliance on informal advice*. Providing off-the-cuff guidance without proper research or documentation can result in clients making poor financial decisions, opening the CPA to liability for negligent misrepresentation.
- *Failure to identify going concern issues*. Auditors who overlook or inadequately disclose a company's financial distress, especially when bankruptcy follows, may be sued for failing to alert stakeholders.
- *Inadequate supervision of staff*. When junior staff make errors that go uncorrected due to a lack of oversight, the supervising CPA can be held liable for negligent supervision.
- *Conflicts of interest*. Failure to disclose relationships or maintain objectivity, especially in audit or attestation engagements, can lead to both professional sanctions and legal claims.

Each of these situations underscores the importance of professional skepticism, clear engagement terms, thorough documentation, and adherence to professional standards in minimizing malpractice risk.

Contract Liability and Legal Defenses

What defenses can a CPA raise against a malpractice claim? In this section, we cover the general types of defenses, along with several related issues.

Nature of a CPA-Client Contractual Relationship

The CPA-client contractual relationship is a legally binding agreement that establishes the scope of services, responsibilities, and expectations between a CPA and their client. This relationship is typically formalized through an engagement letter, which outlines the nature of the services to be provided – such as tax preparation, audit services, or consulting – along with deliverables, timelines, fees, and any limitations. The engagement letter is critical, as it helps define the professional duties assumed by the CPA and limits the expectations of the client. By doing so, it provides a framework for accountability and helps prevent misunderstandings that can lead to legal disputes.

From a malpractice perspective, the CPA-client contract plays a central role in determining whether a breach of duty has occurred. Malpractice claims arise when a CPA fails to perform according to the standard of care expected of a reasonably prudent professional, and that failure results in harm to the client. The engagement letter or service agreement becomes a primary reference point for establishing what services the CPA agreed to provide and whether the alleged negligence falls within the scope of that agreement. If the CPA deviated from the terms or omitted critical steps implied by professional standards, they may be held liable for damages.

Moreover, the contractual relationship may impose additional duties that are not explicitly stated but which are implied by the nature of the professional engagement, such as confidentiality, loyalty, and timely communication. Courts often look at both express and implied duties when evaluating whether a CPA exercised due professional care. A well-drafted engagement letter can serve as a defense tool by narrowing the scope of responsibilities and excluding services not agreed upon, which could otherwise expose the CPA to broader liability.

In litigation, the presence or absence of a clear written agreement can influence whether the case proceeds under a breach of contract or tort theory. In breach of contract claims, the client must prove that the CPA failed to meet agreed-upon obligations. In tort-based malpractice, the focus shifts to a failure to meet general professional standards, regardless of contract terms. Consequently, a clearly articulated CPA-client agreement not only guides the professional relationship but also serves as vital evidence in defending against malpractice claims, highlighting the importance of precision and clarity in client engagements.

Types of Breaches

In a CPA-client contractual relationship, several types of breaches can occur, each potentially giving rise to malpractice claims or breach of contract lawsuits. These breaches generally fall into categories related to timing, scope of services, deliverables, and professional standards.

Timing breaches involve a CPA's failure to meet agreed-upon deadlines for completing work. For example, if a CPA commits to filing a client's tax return by a statutory deadline but submits it late, resulting in penalties, the client may pursue damages. Even in non-deadline-sensitive engagements, unreasonable delays can harm a client's ability to make timely business or financial decisions. Courts may consider whether delays were avoidable and whether the CPA communicated effectively about any obstacles.

Scope breaches occur when a CPA performs services that deviate from what was contractually agreed upon, either by omitting required tasks or by taking actions beyond the authorized engagement. For example, if a CPA is hired solely to prepare compiled financial statements but instead provides what appears to be an audit or review, this could mislead third parties and expose the CPA to unintended liability. Likewise, if a CPA omits key procedures, such as failing to reconcile accounts when providing bookkeeping services, they may be seen as breaching the agreed scope of work.

Deliverable breaches arise when a CPA fails to provide the work product as described in the engagement letter or agreement. This might include incomplete reports, inaccurate tax returns, or substandard financial statements. Deliverables must meet not only contractual specifications but also adhere to professional standards. A poorly executed audit or a materially misstated tax return can be grounds for both a breach of contract and a negligence claim.

Additional breaches can involve a failure to maintain client confidentiality, lack of communication, or errors in billing. In some cases, the CPA might improperly terminate the engagement without sufficient notice, causing disruption or harm to the client.

Ultimately, the significance of any breach is judged in the context of the damages it causes and the expectations set in the original agreement. Detailed engagement letters, regular updates, and adherence to professional guidelines help minimize the risk of such breaches and serve as key protections for both parties if disputes arise. A clearly defined and carefully managed contractual relationship is essential to reducing malpractice exposure.

Defenses

When faced with a claim of breach of contract or professional malpractice, a CPA has several viable defenses that can be used to reduce or eliminate liability. These defenses include the absence of a contractual duty, client interference or misrepresentation, contributory negligence, and the expiration of the statute of limitations. Each of these defenses challenges an essential element of the client's claim and can form a strong basis for dismissal or mitigation of damages. In more detail:

- *Lack of contractual duty.* One of the most fundamental defenses is that the CPA had no contractual obligation to perform the service that is alleged to have been deficient. If there was no written or implied agreement between the CPA and the plaintiff for a specific service, then no enforceable duty existed. This is particularly relevant when clients assert liability for tasks that were outside the scope of the original engagement. A clearly written engagement letter can support this defense by outlining exactly what services were agreed upon, as well as any excluded services. If the CPA did not undertake a duty in the first place, they cannot be held liable for its alleged breach.

- *Client interference or misrepresentation.* CPAs can also defend against liability by showing that the client interfered with the performance of the engagement or provided misleading, incomplete, or false information. For instance, if a client fails to disclose all necessary financial records, deliberately omits liabilities, or conceals material facts, the CPA may not be able to complete the engagement properly. In such cases, the CPA may argue that any deficiencies in the work product were directly caused by the client's misconduct or obstruction. Courts are generally less inclined to find CPAs liable when the client's own behavior impaired the CPA's ability to fulfill the contract.

- *Contributory or comparative negligence.* A CPA may also assert that the client's own negligence contributed to the damages suffered. In jurisdictions recognizing contributory or comparative negligence, liability may be reduced or eliminated depending on the extent to which the client's actions caused or exacerbated the harm. For example, if a client ignored tax advice, failed to review drafts, or delayed providing documentation, they may share responsibility for any resulting penalties or errors.

- *Statute of limitations*. Finally, CPAs can invoke the statute of limitations as a defense. Every jurisdiction imposes a time limit within which a client must bring a legal action for breach of contract. If the client files a claim after this period has expired, the CPA can seek dismissal on procedural grounds. The statute of limitations typically begins when the alleged breach occurs or, in some jurisdictions, when the client discovers the breach. Promptly documenting the end of an engagement and maintaining engagement letters and workpapers can be crucial in asserting this defense.

Together, these defenses underscore the importance of professional boundaries, written agreements, and proactive communication. They provide CPAs with important legal tools to shield themselves from unfair or unfounded contract liability claims.

Damages in Contract and Tort Claims

What kind of damages can a CPA expect from an adverse malpractice judgment? In this section, we cover the types of damages, how expert testimony can be used to assess the amount of damages, and how limitation of liability clauses can be used to mitigate these damages.

Types of Damages

In malpractice cases against CPAs, the types of damages a plaintiff may seek generally fall under three main categories, which are compensatory, consequential, and punitive. The classification and availability of these damages depend on whether the claim is based on contract law or tort law. More specifically:

- *Compensatory damages*. Compensatory damages are the most commonly awarded in malpractice cases and are intended to make the injured party whole by reimbursing them for direct losses incurred as a result of the CPA's misconduct. In contract-based claims, these damages are typically limited to the losses directly resulting from the breach of the CPA's obligations under the engagement letter or service agreement. For example, if a CPA failed to file a tax return on time, the client may recover late penalties and interest as compensatory damages. In tort-based claims, such as negligence, compensatory damages include not only the direct financial loss but may also include other harm proximately caused by the CPA's breach of the professional duty of care. This might involve, for instance, the cost of correcting a faulty audit or the diminished value of a business that relied on inaccurate financial statements.
- *Consequential damages*. Consequential damages compensate for losses that extend beyond the immediate contract or direct professional action, as long as they were reasonably foreseeable at the time the contract was formed or the negligent act occurred. In a CPA malpractice case, this might include lost

profits, loss of business opportunities, or reputational damage resulting from reliance on incorrect financial reports. In contract cases, courts generally apply a foreseeability standard, meaning the CPA is only liable for damages that could reasonably be anticipated. In tort claims, the standard is similar but based on proximate cause – which is whether the damages can be directly traced to the negligent act.

- *Punitive damages.* Punitive damages are rarely awarded in CPA malpractice cases, but they may be available in tort actions where the CPA's conduct was not merely negligent but rose to the level of fraud, malice, or gross recklessness. For example, if a CPA intentionally falsifies financial statements or knowingly assists a client in committing tax fraud, a court may impose punitive damages to punish the behavior and deter similar misconduct. Courts typically do not allow punitive damages in breach of contract cases, as the goal of contract law is to enforce promises rather than to punish. However, if the breach is accompanied by egregious misconduct that overlaps with a tort, punitive damages may be considered.

In summary, damages in malpractice cases against CPAs vary significantly, depending on the legal theory pursued. Compensatory and consequential damages are most common, while punitive damages are reserved for the most serious ethical violations.

Comparison of Damages in Tort vs. Contract

When a malpractice claim is brought against a CPA, the legal theory under which the claim is pursued, tort or contract, significantly influences the types and extent of damages that may be awarded. Although both approaches seek to address harm caused by the CPA's misconduct, they differ in focus, scope, and remedial objectives.

In a contract-based malpractice claim, damages are primarily guided by the principle of *expectation interest*, aiming to place the injured client in the position they would have been in had the contract been properly performed. These damages are typically limited to those foreseeable at the time of contracting, such as professional fees paid, penalties for late filings, or other direct losses outlined in the engagement agreement. Consequential damages may be recoverable, but only if they were reasonably contemplated by both parties during contract formation. Courts are generally reluctant to award damages for reputational harm or lost business opportunities in contract claims, unless such outcomes were explicitly addressed in the agreement.

By contrast, a tort-based claim, which is typically grounded in negligence, focuses on whether the CPA breached a duty of care owed to the client or a third party, resulting in harm. Tort law allows for broader recovery, including both economic and non-economic losses, provided they can be causally linked to the CPA's actions. Compensatory damages in tort may cover not only direct financial losses but also indirect losses, such as diminished business value or costs incurred to correct the CPA's errors. Additionally, courts may consider reputational damage and emotional distress under certain circumstances, though these are less common in purely financial malpractice cases.

Another key distinction lies in the potential for punitive damages. While punitive damages are generally not recoverable in contract law, they may be awarded in tort claims where the CPA's conduct involves fraud, gross negligence, or willful misconduct. This serves a punitive and deterrent function, particularly when the CPA has intentionally deceived a client or engaged in unethical behavior.

In short, contract claims are more limited and focus on the specific terms of the engagement, while tort claims allow for broader, fault-based recovery. Plaintiffs pursuing malpractice claims against CPAs often allege both tort and contract theories simultaneously, maximizing the potential for recovery by encompassing both foreseeable contractual harms and broader negligence-related losses.

Limitation of Liability Clauses in Engagement Letters

Limitation of liability clauses in engagement letters are contractual provisions used by CPAs to reduce or cap their potential exposure to malpractice claims. These clauses typically restrict the amount of damages a client may recover, often limiting recovery to the amount of fees paid for services or excluding certain types of damages, such as consequential or punitive damages.

From a malpractice standpoint, these clauses serve as a risk management tool, allowing CPAs to define and contain their legal obligations in advance. By incorporating clear terms in the engagement letter, a CPA can attempt to shift some of the litigation risk associated with professional services. This is particularly important in high-risk engagements where errors or client misinterpretations could result in significant claims.

However, the enforceability of limitation of liability clauses depends on state law and judicial interpretation. Courts will generally uphold such clauses if they are clearly written, mutually agreed upon, and not contrary to public policy. Some jurisdictions may refuse to enforce them in cases involving gross negligence, fraud, or willful misconduct, as public policy often dictates that professionals should not be able to shield themselves from liability arising from egregious conduct.

In malpractice litigation, the presence of a valid limitation of liability clause may significantly reduce a CPA's financial exposure. It can also influence settlement negotiations by narrowing the scope of recoverable damages. Nonetheless, such clauses do not eliminate a CPA's duty of care or absolve them from professional responsibility. Clients still expect competent service, and courts may scrutinize the clause closely to ensure it does not unfairly disadvantage the client.

In conclusion, while limitation of liability clauses are a valuable protective mechanism for CPAs, their effectiveness is contingent on careful drafting, client consent, and legal enforceability.

Sample Limitation of Liability Clause

To the fullest extent permitted by applicable law and professional standards, the total liability of [CPA Firm Name], its partners, employees, and agents for any and all claims, losses, costs, or damages arising out of this engagement shall be limited to the total fees paid to [CPA Firm Name] for the services rendered under this engagement letter. In no event shall [CPA Firm Name] be liable for any special, incidental, indirect, or consequential damages, including without limitation, loss of profits, data, or business opportunities, even if advised of the possibility of such damages.

Always consult legal counsel before including or enforcing a limitation of liability clause. Some jurisdictions or professional regulations (e.g., the AICPA Code of Professional Conduct) may limit or disallow liability waivers in certain types of engagements, such as audits. This clause is generally more appropriate in consulting or tax preparation engagements than assurance services.

Role of Expert Testimony in Damage Assessment

In malpractice claims against CPAs, expert testimony plays a critical role in the assessment of damages. Given the technical nature of accounting services and the complexity of financial harm, courts and juries often rely on expert witnesses to interpret facts, quantify losses, and establish causation between the CPA's conduct and the alleged damages.

Expert testimony is especially vital in demonstrating the standard of care, a threshold that must be met to prove negligence or professional misconduct. However, once liability is established, experts are instrumental in calculating the monetary impact of the CPA's actions. This involves analyzing financial statements, tax returns, audit trails, and market data to determine how the CPA's error directly or indirectly caused financial loss. Experts often reconstruct "what-if" scenarios to show how the client's financial position would have differed had the CPA performed competently.

In contract-based malpractice claims, experts may help assess direct damages, such as fees paid for faulty services or costs incurred to remedy the CPA's mistake. In tort-based claims, expert testimony becomes even more crucial, as the calculation of damages may include more speculative elements like lost profits, business valuation losses, or reputational harm. The expert must isolate the damages attributable to the CPA's conduct from other external factors, ensuring the damages are not overstated.

Courts generally require that damage calculations meet a standard of reasonable certainty, not mere speculation. Thus, an expert's credibility, methodology, and use of reliable data are all scrutinized. For example, valuation experts may be called in to measure economic loss using established models, such as discounted cash flows or market comparables. Tax experts may be needed to quantify penalties and interest due to improper filings.

Moreover, expert witnesses can also challenge the opposing party's damage estimates, highlighting flaws in assumptions or methodologies. In doing so, they can significantly affect the outcome of the case by limiting or disproving alleged losses.

Ultimately, expert testimony serves both an explanatory and evidentiary function, translating complex financial information into a form the court can understand and rely on. In CPA malpractice cases, the presence of expert analysis is often decisive in determining not only the amount of damages awarded but whether damages can be proven at all.

CPA Malpractice Litigation Consequences

What is the impact of an adverse malpractice claim? In this section, we address all possible impacts, including financial losses, insurance coverage issues, professional sanctions, reputational harm, the loss of clients, and so forth.

Financial Liability and Insurance Coverage Implications

A CPA facing a malpractice claim may encounter significant financial liability, which can stem from legal defense costs, settlements, or court-ordered damages. These liabilities can threaten the CPA's personal and firm assets if not adequately managed or insured.

To mitigate such risks, most CPAs maintain professional liability insurance, commonly known as errors and omissions (E&O) insurance. This coverage is designed specifically to protect against claims of professional negligence. It typically covers legal defense costs, settlements, and judgments, subject to policy limits and exclusions. Policies may also include coverage for regulatory investigations, subpoena response assistance, and reputational harm. However, coverage is not universal; most policies exclude claims arising from criminal acts, intentional fraud, or services rendered outside the scope of the insured's profession.

The scope of insurance protection depends on key policy elements, including the retroactive date, policy limits, and deductible. Claims-made policies, which are standard for malpractice coverage, require that both the incident and the claim occur while the policy is active. A lapse in coverage can expose the CPA to uncovered liability, even for services provided during an insured period. Therefore, maintaining continuous coverage and considering tail coverage after retirement or business closure is critical.

Additionally, insurers may settle claims to avoid higher litigation costs, even without the CPA's admission of wrongdoing. This can impact a CPA's professional standing, licensure, or future insurability. CPAs must also be aware of reporting obligations, as a failure to notify the insurer of a potential claim promptly may void coverage.

In summary, financial liability in malpractice claims can be substantial, but appropriate insurance coverage is a vital risk management tool that helps protect a CPA's financial and professional future.

Professional Sanctions and Licensing Board Actions

When a CPA is implicated in a malpractice claim, professional sanctions and licensing board actions may follow if the conduct in question breaches ethical or professional standards. These consequences are separate from civil liability and stem from the regulatory authority of state boards of accountancy, the AICPA, and other professional oversight bodies. Their primary concern is protecting the public interest and maintaining the integrity of the accounting profession.

Licensing boards investigate malpractice allegations to determine whether a CPA violated state statutes, administrative rules, or professional conduct standards. Even if a civil malpractice lawsuit is settled or dismissed, boards can still impose disciplinary measures if they find evidence of incompetence, gross negligence, fraud, or unethical behavior. Typical actions include formal reprimands, fines, mandatory continuing education, probation, license suspension, or permanent license revocation. The severity of the sanction typically correlates with the nature and extent of the CPA's misconduct, as well as whether the violation was a first-time or repeat offense.

Additionally, membership organizations such as the AICPA may impose their own sanctions under the Code of Professional Conduct. If a CPA is found to have violated ethical principles, such as due care, objectivity, or integrity, they may face suspension or expulsion from the organization. These sanctions can damage a CPA's reputation and diminish professional credibility, even if the individual retains state licensure.

Disciplinary proceedings generally begin with a complaint, followed by an investigation and a formal hearing. CPAs are entitled to due process, including the opportunity to respond to allegations and present a defense. However, cooperation with the board and demonstration of corrective action may mitigate disciplinary outcomes.

Sanctions are often publicly disclosed, which can impact a CPA's ability to attract and retain clients or obtain future employment. Therefore, avoiding professional discipline requires not only compliance with technical standards, but also a proactive commitment to ethical behavior and quality control.

In short, malpractice claims can trigger serious regulatory consequences that go beyond financial liability, potentially endangering a CPA's professional license and long-term career.

Reputational Harm and Client Loss

A malpractice charge against a CPA can lead to significant reputational harm and client loss, even before any legal liability is determined. In the accounting profession, trust and credibility are fundamental assets. A single malpractice allegation, whether substantiated or not, can erode client confidence and damage a CPA's standing in the professional community. Reputational damage may stem from public disclosure of the claim, negative media coverage, disciplinary proceedings, or public sanctions by licensing boards or the AICPA.

Current clients may respond to a malpractice charge by reducing the scope of their engagement, seeking alternative service providers, or terminating the relationship entirely. Prospective clients, when conducting due diligence, may view the allegation as a red flag, especially in sensitive areas such as audit, tax compliance, or forensic services. This loss of business not only affects revenue but may also impact the firm's future growth, referrals, and ability to bid for high-value contracts.

Beyond client attrition, reputational harm can have broader consequences. A CPA may face increased scrutiny from regulators, banks, and insurers. Professional liability insurance premiums may rise, and coverage may become more restrictive. Additionally, other professionals, such as attorneys or financial advisors, may be reluctant to collaborate with a CPA whose credibility has been compromised.

Rebuilding a tarnished reputation is difficult and time-consuming. It often requires public statements, corrective actions, enhanced quality control procedures, and a long-term demonstration of ethical behavior and professional competence. Even with these efforts, a CPA's name may remain associated with the malpractice claim in regulatory records and online databases.

Importantly, reputational damage often occurs regardless of the outcome of the malpractice case. Mere allegations can trigger doubt among clients and peers, reinforcing the importance of preventative risk management. CPAs must invest in strong internal controls, client communication practices, and ethical compliance to safeguard their reputation. In short, reputational harm from a malpractice charge can lead to lasting financial and professional consequences, making it one of the most damaging aspects of a CPA's legal exposure.

Effects on Firm-Wide Risk Management

When a CPA within a firm is charged with malpractice, the impact extends beyond the individual to the entire organization's risk management framework. Such an event exposes systemic vulnerabilities and often prompts a firm-wide reassessment of its policies, controls, and professional standards. The malpractice charge may reveal gaps in supervision, documentation, training, or client acceptance procedures, indicating that existing safeguards failed to prevent or detect problematic conduct.

In response, the firm is likely to undertake a comprehensive internal review to identify the root causes and implement corrective measures. This may include revising engagement review protocols, strengthening quality control systems, enhancing conflict-of-interest checks, and introducing more rigorous peer reviews. Firms may also expand staff training on ethics, independence, and adherence to professional standards to reduce the likelihood of future claims. These actions, while necessary, require time, financial resources, and management attention, potentially diverting the firm's focus from business development and client service.

A malpractice charge can also affect the firm's external relationships. Insurance carriers may raise premiums or impose more restrictive terms on the firm's professional liability coverage. Clients may seek reassurance that proper oversight exists at all organizational levels, and some may reduce or terminate engagements due to perceived reputational risk. Recruiting and retaining talent can also become more difficult, as top candidates may hesitate to join a firm under scrutiny.

Additionally, the firm may experience heightened regulatory oversight. State boards or professional bodies could require periodic reporting, additional compliance steps, or independent monitoring. If the CPA in question was a partner or principal, questions may arise regarding the firm's governance, tone at the top, and accountability structures.

In summary, a malpractice charge against one CPA can disrupt a firm's entire risk management posture. It serves as a catalyst for structural improvements but also presents reputational, operational, and financial challenges. Proactive, transparent management of the incident, and a clear commitment to raising professional standards, are essential for maintaining client trust and long-term firm stability.

Personal Stress, Time Loss, and Emotional Impact

A malpractice charge can impose intense personal stress, significant time loss, and deep emotional impact on a CPA. These effects often begin the moment a claim is filed, regardless of its validity or eventual outcome. For many professionals, being accused of negligence strikes at the core of their identity, challenging their integrity, competence, and long-standing client relationships. The resulting psychological burden may manifest as anxiety, sleeplessness, reduced self-esteem, and, in severe cases, depression or burnout.

Defending against a malpractice claim consumes time and attention that would otherwise be devoted to serving clients or managing the business. A CPA may be required to gather extensive documentation, consult with legal counsel, and participate in depositions, hearings, or settlement discussions. These tasks are often drawn out over months or years, creating a prolonged period of uncertainty. The ongoing distraction can impair work performance, lead to billing losses, and disrupt the continuity of service to other clients.

The emotional toll is compounded by fear of reputational damage, financial liability, and regulatory consequences. CPAs often fear losing their license, tarnishing their professional legacy, or being viewed as unreliable by clients and peers. If the matter becomes public, media coverage or disciplinary board notices can amplify embarrassment and stress. Personal relationships may also suffer, as the CPA's emotional distress spills into family life or social interactions.

Furthermore, even if the CPA is ultimately cleared of wrongdoing, the experience can leave lasting scars. Many professionals report a diminished sense of trust in clients or colleagues, increased reluctance to take on higher-risk engagements, and a general loss of confidence in their professional judgment.

To cope, some CPAs turn to support from peers, legal advisors, or mental health professionals. However, the stigma surrounding malpractice claims may discourage open discussion, leading to isolation.

In sum, a malpractice charge is not just a legal or financial issue, it is a profoundly personal ordeal that can disrupt every facet of a CPA's life. Audit firms should recognize this human cost and offer appropriate support mechanisms when such events occur.

Specific High-Risk Scenarios for Litigation

There are a few areas in which a lack of attention by a CPA is more likely to result in malpractice claims. We discuss five of these areas in the following pages.

Altering or Omitting Material Financial Statement Disclosures

Altering or omitting material financial statement disclosures is one of the highest-risk scenarios for malpractice litigation faced by CPAs. Financial statement disclosures are essential for ensuring transparency, full and fair presentation, and compliance with generally accepted accounting principles. When a CPA alters, withholds, or omits these disclosures, either deliberately or through negligence, the result may be materially misleading financial statements. Investors, creditors, regulators, and other users rely on these disclosures to make informed decisions, and any deficiency can significantly distort their understanding of a company's financial position or performance.

The risk of litigation arises primarily when a CPA's failure to ensure adequate disclosure leads to financial losses by third parties who relied on the statements. Courts have held CPAs to a professional standard that includes the duty to detect and communicate material misstatements, including those related to omitted disclosures. The risk increases further if the CPA is found to have been complicit in altering disclosures to mask unfavorable conditions, such as pending litigation, debt covenant violations, related-party transactions, or going concern uncertainties. Such actions may be viewed not only as negligence but potentially as fraudulent misrepresentation, which can expose the CPA to punitive damages and criminal liability.

Professional standards stress the importance of disclosure integrity. Auditors are required to obtain sufficient evidence that disclosures are complete and presented in accordance with the applicable reporting framework. Failure to do so can result in sanctions, license suspension, or expulsion from professional bodies. Moreover, civil lawsuits may allege breach of contract, negligence, or even securities law violations if the financial statements were part of a public filing.

The CPA's responsibility does not end with client instructions – independence and professional skepticism are key. If a client requests the omission of certain disclosures to present a more favorable financial image, the CPA must resist such pressure and, if necessary, resign from the engagement. Courts typically look unfavorably on CPAs who prioritize client retention over professional ethics.

In sum, the alteration or omission of material financial disclosures undermines the very credibility of the financial reporting process. For CPAs, such conduct significantly increases exposure to malpractice claims, damages, regulatory action, and irreparable reputational harm. The best protection lies in strict adherence to professional standards, thorough documentation, and the exercise of independent judgment.

Misreporting Income or Deductions in Tax Returns

Misreporting income or deductions on tax returns is a high-risk scenario for malpractice litigation against a CPA, as it directly violates federal and state tax laws and breaches the duty of care owed to clients and taxing authorities. Whether the misreporting arises from negligence, willful disregard of IRS regulations, or complicity in a client's scheme to underreport taxes, the CPA may face severe civil and potentially criminal liability. Errors that result in underpayment of taxes, substantial penalties, or triggering of IRS audits can quickly lead to accusations of malpractice if the CPA failed to exercise due diligence or professional judgment.

One of the most common grounds for tax-related malpractice claims is the CPA's failure to detect or appropriately advise a client on income recognition, deduction eligibility, or documentation requirements. For example, improperly classifying personal expenses as business deductions or omitting income from foreign sources without disclosure can constitute a material misstatement. Clients often rely heavily on their CPA's expertise in navigating complex tax regulations, and any error that results in penalties or additional tax assessments may prompt legal action. Even when the misreporting stems from incomplete or misleading information provided by the client, the CPA is expected to exercise professional skepticism and, where applicable, make reasonable inquiries.

Malpractice risk is further heightened if the CPA's actions violate IRS Circular 230 or the AICPA's Statements on Standards for Tax Services. These standards require CPAs to make reasonable efforts to obtain the necessary facts, apply the law correctly, and avoid taking positions that lack substantial authority. Failure to meet these obligations may result in disciplinary action by the IRS Office of Professional Responsibility, suspension of practice rights, or referral for criminal investigation in egregious cases.

From a legal perspective, tax-related malpractice claims typically involve allegations of negligence, breach of fiduciary duty, or misrepresentation. Plaintiffs may seek compensatory damages, including interest and penalties assessed by tax authorities, costs of amended returns, and legal fees. Additionally, in cases involving fraud or gross negligence, punitive damages may also be awarded.

In summary, misreporting income or deductions exposes CPAs to serious malpractice risk. To mitigate exposure, CPAs must adhere strictly to ethical standards, maintain comprehensive documentation, communicate clearly with clients, and refuse to participate in or overlook improper tax reporting. Professional integrity and due diligence remain the best defenses against liability.

Accepting Unverifiable Client Representations

Accepting unverifiable client representations without appropriate corroboration is a significant malpractice risk for CPAs, as it undermines the reliability of financial statements and tax filings, and potentially facilitates fraud or misreporting. CPAs have a professional obligation to exercise due care, professional skepticism, and adhere to standards that require independent verification of material information. When a CPA relies solely on a client's oral or undocumented assertions, such as undocumented expenses, unrecorded liabilities, or unverifiable asset valuations, they risk issuing work that contains material misstatements, which can lead to financial loss for users of the information and expose the CPA to legal liability.

In both audit and tax engagements, professional standards emphasize the importance of corroborative evidence. Auditing standards specifically caution against overreliance on management representations and require CPAs to obtain sufficient appropriate audit evidence. Similarly, the AICPA's Statements on Standards for Tax Services require CPAs to make reasonable inquiries when a client's claims appear implausible, inconsistent, or lack necessary documentation. Ignoring these standards increases the likelihood of errors, client disputes, and third-party lawsuits, particularly if the information was relied upon by lenders, investors, or tax authorities.

Malpractice claims arising from this scenario often allege negligence, misrepresentation, or breach of fiduciary duty. For example, if a CPA accepts inflated revenue numbers or undocumented deductions and these figures are later audited and disallowed, the client may sue for penalties, interest, back taxes, or business losses stemming from reliance on the CPA's work. In litigation, courts assess whether the CPA adhered to the applicable professional standards and acted as a reasonably prudent practitioner would under similar circumstances. Failing to document due diligence or obtain supporting evidence can lead to unfavorable outcomes for the CPA.

Furthermore, accepting unverifiable representations may also trigger regulatory scrutiny or disciplinary action by licensing boards or professional bodies. Sanctions can include fines, license suspension, or expulsion, particularly if the CPA's conduct is deemed to have enabled fraud or materially misstated financial reports.

To avoid such liability, CPAs must remain vigilant in applying professional skepticism, insist on documentation when necessary, and clearly communicate to clients the limitations of unverified information. When supporting evidence is unavailable, the CPA should disclose this fact appropriately or decline to provide assurance services.

Ignoring Internal Whistleblower Alerts

Ignoring internal whistleblower alerts represents a high-risk malpractice scenario for a CPA, as it reflects a failure to respond to credible indicators of potential fraud, misstatement, or internal control deficiencies. Whistleblower reports often arise from employees or insiders who have direct knowledge of irregularities or unethical practices. When a CPA disregards such alerts without proper investigation or documentation, they expose themselves to claims of negligence, professional misconduct, or willful blindness.

Professional standards require CPAs to exercise professional skepticism and to follow up on red flags that may indicate material misstatements or violations of law. The AICPA's auditing standards emphasize that auditors must consider the reliability of information from internal sources, including whistleblower complaints, especially when these involve allegations of management override, financial statement manipulation, or regulatory noncompliance. A CPA who fails to assess such reports may be deemed to have violated their duty of care, particularly if the concerns later prove valid and result in financial loss, regulatory sanctions, or reputational damage to stakeholders.

From a litigation standpoint, ignoring whistleblower alerts can be interpreted as gross negligence or reckless disregard of professional responsibilities. Plaintiffs, whether clients, shareholders, creditors, or regulators, may argue that the CPA had a duty to investigate known risks and failed to take appropriate action, leading to avoidable harm. In such cases, courts are likely to consider whether a reasonably prudent auditor would have responded differently, and whether earlier intervention could have prevented fraud or misreporting.

To reduce exposure, CPAs must take whistleblower alerts seriously by documenting receipt, evaluating the credibility of the claims, and initiating an appropriate investigative or audit response. Even if the allegations prove unsubstantiated, showing that due diligence was performed demonstrates adherence to professional standards. In essence, responsiveness to internal warnings is not only a best practice but also a safeguard against malpractice liability and reputational harm.

Performing Attest Services Without Adequate Independence

Performing attest services without adequate independence is a high-risk malpractice scenario for a CPA because it compromises the integrity of the engagement, violates professional standards, and undermines public trust in the financial reporting process. Independence, both in fact and in appearance, is a fundamental requirement for all attest engagements, including audits, reviews, and examinations. When a CPA lacks independence due to financial, familial, or managerial relationships with the client, or through the provision of conflicting non-attest services, the credibility of their opinion is severely impaired. Any material misstatement, fraud, or error that arises under these circumstances can lead to malpractice claims, even if the CPA was unaware of the issue.

The AICPA Code of Professional Conduct clearly defines circumstances that impair independence and prohibit CPAs from issuing audit opinions when such conditions exist. If a CPA issues an opinion on financial statements while lacking independence, users of those statements may suffer financial harm from relying on what they believed was an objective assessment. Should such users experience losses, they may bring malpractice suits against the CPA, alleging negligence, misrepresentation, or failure to meet professional standards.

Courts and regulators tend to view violations of independence with particular severity, because independence is considered the foundation of an attest professional's credibility. Even if the CPA conducted the engagement competently, the lack of independence itself may be sufficient grounds for liability, as it represents a breach of ethical and legal obligations. Furthermore, clients may sue the CPA if a non-independent audit leads to the disallowance of financial filings, restatements, or regulatory penalties.

Regulatory consequences are also substantial. CPAs found to have violated independence rules may face investigations by state boards of accountancy, potentially resulting in fines, suspension of practice rights, or permanent disbarment from practicing before regulatory bodies.

To mitigate this risk, CPAs must rigorously assess potential conflicts before accepting or continuing attest engagements. This includes maintaining strict separation between consulting and auditing functions, avoiding financial entanglements, and disclosing any relationships that could impair objectivity. Adequate documentation and internal reviews of independence compliance are essential. In summary, failing to maintain independence places the CPA at significant risk of malpractice litigation, professional sanctions, and irreparable damage to reputation.

Use of Unqualified Staff or Subcontractors

The use of unqualified staff or subcontractors in the performance of professional accounting services is a high-risk scenario for malpractice litigation against a CPA. CPAs have a duty to ensure that all individuals working under their supervision possess the requisite competence, training, and ethical standards to perform their assigned tasks in accordance with applicable professional guidelines. Delegating audit, tax, or advisory responsibilities to individuals lacking appropriate qualifications can result in errors, omissions, or noncompliance with professional standards, which may ultimately lead to client losses and subsequent legal claims.

Professional standards require CPAs to exercise due care in planning and supervising work, regardless of whether the work is performed by employees, subcontractors, or outsourced service providers. This includes assessing the qualifications, technical knowledge, and experience of the personnel assigned to tasks. When unqualified individuals perform procedures without proper oversight, the likelihood of inaccuracies in financial reporting, tax filings, or compliance evaluations increases significantly.

Malpractice claims may arise if a client suffers harm as a result of negligent performance by unqualified staff. For example, if a junior staff member improperly tests internal controls due to inadequate training, and fraud later occurs that could have been prevented with proper procedures, the CPA firm may be held liable. Even if the CPA was not directly involved in the mistake, courts often impose liability based on supervisory negligence, especially when there is a failure to implement adequate quality control policies.

The risk is particularly acute in engagements that require specialized knowledge, such as those involving complex tax regulations, industry-specific accounting rules, or advanced auditing techniques. Using underqualified personnel in such situations not only increases the risk of error but may also constitute a breach of the engagement contract or a violation of professional ethics.

In addition to civil litigation, regulators and licensing boards may investigate the CPA for violating rules related to competency, supervision, and quality control. Consequences can include censure, fines, license suspension, or expulsion from professional associations.

To mitigate this risk, CPAs must conduct thorough evaluations of all staff and subcontractors, provide appropriate training, and ensure proper supervision and review of all work performed. By maintaining rigorous internal quality controls, CPAs can safeguard client interests and protect themselves against malpractice exposure stemming from unqualified personnel.

EXAMPLE

A notable case involving CPA malpractice due to client-altered financial statements is *Cenco Inc. v. Seidman & Seidman*, decided by the Seventh Circuit Court of Appeals in 1982. In this case, Cenco Inc., a manufacturer of optical equipment, engaged Seidman & Seidman, a national accounting firm, to audit its financial statements. Over several years, senior management at Cenco conspired to inflate inventory values and manipulate financial results to enhance the company's stock price and secure financing. The fraud was eventually discovered, leading to financial losses and shareholder lawsuits.

Cenco subsequently sued Seidman & Seidman for negligence and malpractice, claiming the auditors failed to detect the fraudulent activities. The case raised significant questions about auditor responsibility when clients actively conceal or falsify information. Cenco alleged that Seidman's failure to detect the inflated inventory figures constituted a breach of duty and contributed to the damages suffered by the company and its shareholders.

However, the court ruled in favor of the accounting firm, emphasizing that the fraud had been perpetrated by the company's senior management and that Cenco, as a corporate entity, could not benefit from its own wrongdoing. The court applied the in pari delicto doctrine, which bars recovery when the plaintiff is equally at fault. It reasoned that because top management orchestrated the fraud, the corporation was not a victim but a participant.

The case is significant in CPA malpractice jurisprudence because it clarified that auditors are not insurers against fraud, particularly when the client's leadership is complicit. While the court did not find Seidman liable, the case reinforced the importance of auditor skepticism, thorough inventory testing, and verifying management representations independently. It also highlighted the limits of liability when client misconduct directly undermines the audit process.

CPA Responsibilities in Error Disclosures to Clients

When a CPA uncovers an error, what responsibilities do they have to disclose the issue to a client? This section addresses how these disclosures should be made, along with several related topics.

When and How to Disclose Discovered Errors

When a CPA discovers an error in work previously performed for a client, prompt and transparent disclosure is essential, both to maintain professional integrity and to mitigate potential malpractice exposure. Errors can range from simple clerical mistakes to significant misstatements that may affect a client's financial decisions, tax liabilities, or regulatory compliance. The AICPA Code of Professional Conduct requires CPAs to act with integrity and due care, and these principles guide the proper response when errors are identified.

Disclosure should begin with a timely internal review to confirm the nature, extent, and implications of the error. If the error is material or could lead to client harm, such as penalties, missed opportunities, or reputational damage, then the CPA must notify the client as soon as reasonably possible. The communication should be made in writing and include a clear description of the error, how it occurred, its potential effects, and any recommended corrective actions. The CPA should avoid assigning blame, speculating on liability, or making assurances that could be construed as admissions of malpractice.

To reduce litigation risks, CPAs should maintain detailed documentation of the discovery, internal discussions, communications with the client, and any remedial steps taken. The CPA should also advise the client on how to correct the error, such as amending tax returns or reissuing financial statements, but should avoid taking unilateral action without client consent. If the CPA is no longer engaged by the client, they may still have an ethical duty to alert the former client of the issue, especially if the error could result in harm.

Failure to disclose known errors can significantly heighten malpractice risk. Courts often view nondisclosure as a breach of the duty of care or fiduciary responsibility, especially when the CPA had an opportunity to inform the client and failed to do so. Proactive disclosure, by contrast, can serve as evidence of professionalism and good faith, potentially reducing liability. If the error results in a claim, early disclosure and remediation may limit damages and support a defense that the CPA acted reasonably under the circumstances.

Client Notification and Correction Protocols

In the context of malpractice claims, a CPA must engage in client notification and correction protocols promptly, systematically, and in accordance with professional standards. The following issues are important:

- *When to notify the client.* A CPA should notify the client as soon as a significant error, misstatement, or noncompliance issue is confirmed. The threshold for notification is typically whether the issue could materially affect financial outcomes, lead to regulatory penalties, or compromise the reliability of reports. Errors discovered during ongoing engagements must be addressed right away, whereas errors found post-engagement may still require notification, especially if they could cause foreseeable harm.
- *How to notify the client.* Notification should be delivered in a timely and professional manner, ideally in writing, to provide a clear, permanent record. The CPA should describe the nature and scope of the error, the potential implications, and suggested corrective steps. The communication should avoid language that implies legal liability or fault.
- *Correction protocols.* The CPA should recommend an appropriate method of correction, such as amending prior-year tax returns, issuing restated financial statements, or adjusting current-period entries. However, any corrective action must be undertaken with client approval and, where applicable, under the guidance of legal counsel. If the client refuses to act, the CPA may need to consider resigning from the engagement and consulting legal or professional bodies regarding further disclosure obligations to third parties.

- *Documenting the process.* To reduce malpractice exposure, the CPA should thoroughly document the discovery of the issue, the analysis of its impact, the communication with the client, and any actions taken. These records can be critical in demonstrating adherence to professional standards if a malpractice claim arises.

In summary, CPAs must approach client notification and correction protocols with urgency, clarity, and professionalism. By doing so, they fulfill ethical responsibilities, maintain client trust, and strengthen their legal position in the event of a malpractice allegation.

Distinction Between Innocent Errors and Negligent Errors

In the context of malpractice claims against CPAs, distinguishing between an *innocent error* and a *negligent error* is critical, as it affects liability, damages, and the outcome of legal proceedings. Both types of errors may result in financial harm to clients, but they differ significantly in their legal and ethical implications.

An *innocent error* refers to a mistake made despite the CPA exercising due care, following professional standards, and acting in good faith. These errors are typically the result of human oversight, reasonable misjudgment, or reliance on incomplete or misleading client information. For example, if a CPA prepares a tax return based on all documentation provided and later learns that the client failed to disclose a material income source, the resulting error may be deemed innocent. Courts often do not hold CPAs liable for such errors if they can demonstrate that they acted competently, documented their work, and had no reason to suspect an issue.

In contrast, a *negligent error* arises when a CPA fails to meet the accepted standard of care expected of a reasonably competent professional under similar circumstances. This includes overlooking material facts, failing to perform required audit procedures, misapplying accounting principles, or not verifying questionable client representations. For example, if a CPA fails to reconcile major discrepancies in financial statements or neglects to investigate a suspicious transaction, this oversight could be construed as negligence. Even without intent to deceive, such conduct may constitute professional malpractice if it deviates from established norms of practice.

The distinction is important because only negligent errors (or worse, reckless or intentional misconduct) generally support a malpractice claim. Plaintiffs must prove that the CPA owed a duty, breached that duty through negligent conduct, and caused financial harm. A defense against malpractice often rests on showing that an error was innocent.

Ultimately, the difference between innocent and negligent error lies in the degree of care exercised by the CPA. While both may produce similar outcomes for the client, only negligent errors involve a failure to adhere to the standards of the profession, thereby triggering potential legal liability. Clear documentation, sound judgment, and adherence to professional guidance are essential for CPAs to defend their actions and distinguish between these two categories in a malpractice context.

AICPA Standard on Error Disclosure (ET Section 1.000.001)

The AICPA provides clear guidance on error disclosure through its Statements on Standards for Tax Services (SSTS) and Code of Professional Conduct, which together establish a CPA's responsibilities when discovering errors in prior work.

Under *SSTS No. 6 – Knowledge of Error*, a CPA who becomes aware of an error or omission in a previously filed tax return or submitted financial document must promptly inform the client of the nature of the error, its implications, and the potential consequences, such as penalties or interest. However, the CPA is *not* permitted to inform the IRS or other third parties without the client's consent, except as required by law. The CPA should encourage the client to correct the error but may not take unilateral corrective action.

Similarly, the AICPA Code of Professional Conduct, particularly the Integrity and Objectivity Rule (ET §1.100.001) and the Due Care Rule (ET §1.300.001), requires CPAs to act with honesty, maintain professional standards, and exercise due diligence. These principles support the duty to disclose errors to clients, especially when such errors could materially affect decisions or compliance.

Importantly, if the client refuses to act on the CPA's recommendation to correct the error, the CPA should consider whether continued professional involvement is ethical or exposes them to legal risk. In some cases, the CPA may need to resign from the engagement to avoid implicit endorsement of the erroneous information.

In summary, AICPA standards obligate CPAs to disclose known errors to clients promptly and professionally, encourage correction, and maintain documentation. While disclosure to third parties is limited, the primary ethical responsibility is to ensure that the client is informed and guided in resolving the issue, thereby reducing the risk of further noncompliance or potential malpractice exposure.

Risk Mitigation and Professional Protection Strategies

Mitigating the risk of a malpractice claim is of great importance to any CPA. In this section, we cover the actions that can be most effective in avoiding claims.

Effective Engagement Letters and Scope Definition

Effective engagement letters and clearly defined scopes of work play a crucial role in mitigating the risk of malpractice claims against CPAs. These documents establish the foundation of the professional relationship and help set client expectations regarding the nature, extent, and limitations of services to be performed. By explicitly outlining the responsibilities of both the CPA and the client, engagement letters help prevent misunderstandings that often give rise to legal disputes.

An engagement letter should specify the type of service being rendered – whether it is an audit, review, compilation, or tax return preparation – and clearly indicate what is excluded from the engagement. This clarification is essential, because clients may assume a broader level of assurance or oversight than what is actually being provided. For example, an audit engagement should define materiality thresholds, identify reliance on client representations, and note that absolute assurance is not provided.

In addition, scope definitions should address any known limitations, such as the client's lack of complete documentation or internal controls, and document any agreed-upon procedures or deliverables. This not only protects the CPA but also encourages the client to fulfill their responsibilities, such as providing accurate and timely information.

In the event of a legal challenge, a well-drafted engagement letter serves as evidence that the CPA's duties were limited to the terms agreed upon. It also provides a defense against claims of negligence by showing that services were performed in accordance with professional standards and the scope of the engagement. Including provisions for dispute resolution, limitation of liability clauses, and acknowledgment of terms by the client can further strengthen the CPA's legal position.

Ultimately, engagement letters and scope definitions are vital tools in managing professional risk, ensuring compliance, and reinforcing the CPA's role as a trusted advisor within clearly established boundaries.

Use of Disclaimers and Limitation of Liability Clauses

Disclaimers and limitation of liability clauses are powerful risk management tools that can help CPAs mitigate the likelihood and severity of malpractice claims. When used effectively within engagement letters and client communications, these provisions help clarify the extent of the CPA's responsibility and reduce exposure to legal liability.

Disclaimers are statements that limit the reliance a client or a third party can place on the CPA's work. For example, in compilation engagements, a disclaimer can state that the CPA has not audited or reviewed the financial information and therefore provides no assurance as to its accuracy. This is especially important in lower-assurance services, where the client might otherwise assume a higher level of scrutiny. Disclaimers may also clarify that the CPA is not responsible for detecting fraud, assessing internal controls, or providing legal advice unless specifically engaged to do so.

Limitation of liability clauses restrict the amount or type of damages a client may recover in the event of a dispute. These clauses may cap damages at the amount of fees paid for the engagement or exclude consequential and punitive damages altogether. By contractually limiting potential recovery, these provisions help protect the CPA from large financial losses that may result from client dissatisfaction, miscommunication, or unforeseen events.

Both types of clauses must be carefully worded and comply with applicable state laws and professional ethical standards. Courts may scrutinize such clauses, particularly if they appear to be unfairly one-sided or were not clearly disclosed. Therefore, it is critical that the language is transparent and that the client acknowledges acceptance, ideally through a signed engagement letter.

While these clauses do not provide absolute immunity from malpractice claims, they are an important component of a CPA's risk management strategy. When combined with clear scope definitions, thorough documentation, and professional diligence, disclaimers and limitation of liability clauses reduce ambiguity, set realistic client expectations, and provide a contractual defense in the event of litigation.

Maintaining Thorough Documentation and Workpapers

Maintaining thorough documentation and detailed workpapers is a critical defense mechanism against malpractice claims for CPAs. These records serve as the primary evidence that the CPA performed services in accordance with applicable professional standards, followed due diligence, and exercised appropriate professional judgment. In the event of a client dispute or legal action, the absence of adequate documentation can severely impair a CPA's ability to defend their actions and decisions.

Well-organized workpapers should clearly reflect the scope of the engagement, procedures performed, findings, conclusions, and communications with the client. For audits and reviews, workpapers must demonstrate compliance with Generally Accepted Auditing Standards or other applicable frameworks. For tax and consulting services, documentation should show the factual basis for advice rendered, including reliance on client-provided data, applicable tax laws, and any assumptions made. These records help establish that the CPA acted reasonably and within the defined boundaries of the engagement.

Documentation also helps mitigate risk by promoting consistency and accuracy throughout the engagement. It facilitates internal reviews, quality control, and continuity in case of staff turnover. When risks or irregularities are identified during the engagement, such as inconsistent client responses or red flags, detailed documentation of those concerns and how they were addressed strengthens the CPA's position should questions arise later.

Importantly, documentation also supports communications with the client, particularly regarding limitations, uncertainties, or responsibilities. For instance, written records of meetings, emails, or memos that confirm the client's responsibility for providing accurate information or the CPA's warnings about potential issues can be decisive in defending against allegations of negligence or misrepresentation.

In legal proceedings, the CPA who can present comprehensive workpapers is far better equipped to demonstrate adherence to professional standards and to counter claims of omission, oversight, or misconduct. Ultimately, thorough documentation not only supports the quality and integrity of the CPA's work but also forms the backbone of a credible and effective legal defense, significantly reducing malpractice exposure.

Regular Ethics and Legal Training

Regular ethics and legal training is a proactive and essential strategy for mitigating the risk of malpractice claims against CPAs. As the legal and regulatory landscape evolves, ongoing education ensures that CPAs remain current on professional standards, ethical obligations, and legal responsibilities – areas that are central to avoiding liability exposure.

Ethics training reinforces the CPA's understanding of core principles such as integrity, objectivity, professional competence, due care, and confidentiality. These principles form the foundation of the AICPA Code of Professional Conduct and are integral to decision-making in complex or ambiguous situations. By revisiting real-world case studies and emerging ethical dilemmas, CPAs can better recognize early warning signs of potential conflicts of interest, undue influence, or lapses in independence, and take corrective action before a situation escalates into a legal issue.

Legal training complements ethics education by familiarizing CPAs with the legal implications of their professional activities. This includes liability arising from breach of contract, negligence, fraud, and violations of state accountancy laws or federal regulations. Training often covers how to structure effective engagement letters, navigate client communications, maintain proper documentation, and adhere to reporting and disclosure obligations, all of which reduce the risk of errors and omissions that can trigger malpractice claims.

Regular training also fosters a culture of compliance within CPA firms, particularly when it is integrated into firm-wide risk management and quality control procedures. It empowers staff at all levels to understand their responsibilities, know when to escalate concerns, and follow appropriate protocols for handling client disputes, suspected fraud, or regulatory inquiries.

In the event of a malpractice claim, a CPA who has maintained current training records can also demonstrate to regulators, courts, or professional boards that they took reasonable steps to stay informed and compliant. This can serve as a mitigating factor in disciplinary proceedings or litigation.

Ultimately, regular ethics and legal training equips CPAs with the knowledge and judgment to prevent misconduct, navigate risk, and uphold the public trust, thereby reducing the likelihood and impact of malpractice claims.

When to Consult Legal Counsel or Withdraw from an Engagement

Knowing when to consult legal counsel or withdraw from an engagement is critical for CPAs seeking to mitigate the risk of malpractice claims. These actions are necessary when a CPA encounters legal ambiguity, ethical conflicts, or client behavior that may expose them to liability or compromised professional standards.

Legal counsel should be consulted immediately when the CPA becomes aware of potential legal issues such as suspected fraud, illegal client acts, whistleblower complaints, or subpoena requests. Early legal guidance ensures that the CPA responds appropriately without breaching confidentiality, obstructing justice, or assuming responsibilities outside their expertise. Legal counsel can also assist in drafting defensible documentation, managing disclosures, and preserving privilege in sensitive matters. Failure to seek counsel in high-risk situations can lead to missteps that later become central in malpractice claims.

Consider withdrawing from an engagement when a client refuses to provide necessary information, submits misleading or fraudulent data, disregards professional advice, or engages in unethical behavior. Continuing an engagement under such conditions not only threatens the integrity of the CPA's work but also increases exposure to legal claims by clients, third parties, or regulators. The CPA must carefully document all efforts to resolve the issue and ensure that the client is informed of the reasons for withdrawal in writing.

Additionally, if the CPA discovers a conflict of interest, a lack of independence, or realizes the firm does not have the expertise or resources to complete the engagement properly, withdrawal may be the most prudent course of action. In all cases, disengagement should be handled professionally, with a formal disengagement letter that outlines completed work, the reason for termination, and any responsibilities the client must assume going forward.

By recognizing high-risk scenarios early and responding with legal support or withdrawal when necessary, CPAs protect themselves from entanglement in unethical or unlawful activities. These actions demonstrate professional judgment, preserve the CPA's reputation, and serve as strong defenses in any future malpractice proceedings.

Summary

This book has provided a comprehensive overview of the legal risks and professional responsibilities facing CPAs. It examined how malpractice arises from negligence, breach of contract, or fraud, and underscored the importance of professional judgment, fiduciary duty, and engagement clarity. The book discussed the role of documentation, internal controls, and adherence to standards in preventing legal exposure. It also explored litigation trends, including expanding third-party liability and regulatory scrutiny. Key legal defenses, case law precedents, and damage assessment techniques were covered in detail. Ultimately, the book equips CPAs with the knowledge to mitigate malpractice risks and uphold the integrity of their professional practice.

Glossary

B

Breach of contract. When a CPA fails to perform services as outlined in a formal agreement, typically an engagement letter.

C

Constructive fraud. When false statements are made without the intent to deceive, but under circumstances where the CPA has a duty to know the truth and fails to exercise reasonable care.

D

Deliverable breach. When a CPA fails to provide the work product as described in an engagement letter or agreement.

Disclaimer. A statement that limits the reliance a client or a third party can place on a CPA's work.

Duty of care. A legal obligation requiring individuals or entities to exercise reasonable care to avoid causing harm to others.

E

Expectation interest. The compensation a party seeks in a contract dispute to be put in the position they would have been in had the contract been fully performed.

F

Fiduciary responsibility. When a CPA is in a position of trust and confidence, acting on behalf of a client's best interests.

I

Innocent error. A mistake made despite a CPA exercising due care, following professional standards, and acting in good faith.

L

Legal exposure. The potential for civil or regulatory liability arising from a CPA's professional conduct.

Limitation of liability. A contractual provision that caps the amount one party must pay to the other for damages or losses arising from a breach or specific legal claims.

M

Malpractice. A situation in which a CPA or other accounting professional fails to perform their duties in accordance with the applicable standards of care, competence, and ethical conduct, resulting in harm or financial loss to a client or third party.

N

Negligent error. When a CPA fails to meet the accepted standard of care expected of a reasonably competent professional under similar circumstances.

O

Ordinary negligence. A general failure to act with the care that a reasonably prudent person would use in similar circumstances.

P

Professional judgment. The application of relevant knowledge, experience, and ethical standards in making decisions or providing opinions in complex or ambiguous situations.

Professional negligence. A failure to exercise the level of care, skill, and diligence that a reasonably prudent CPA would exhibit under comparable professional circumstances.

R

Reasonable care. Whether a CPA acted in a manner consistent with what another reasonably prudent professional would have done under similar circumstances.

Reasonable foreseeability. A legal concept that a person should have anticipated the potential consequences of their actions or omissions as likely or probable outcomes.

S

Scope breach. When a CPA performs services that deviate from what was contractually agreed upon, either by omitting required tasks or by taking actions beyond the authorized engagement.

T

Timing breach. A CPA's failure to meet agreed-upon deadlines for completing work.

Index

www.ingramcontent.com/pod-product-compliance
Lightning Source LLC
Chambersburg PA
CBHW080722220326
41520CB00056B/7365